Protestant Episcopal Church USA

Constitution of the Protestant Episcopal Church in the Confederate States of America

and digest of the canons adopted in General Council, in Augusta, Georgia,

November 1862 - Vol. 1

Protestant Episcopal Church USA

Constitution of the Protestant Episcopal Church in the Confederate States of America
and digest of the canons adopted in General Council, in Augusta, Georgia, November 1862 - Vol. 1

ISBN/EAN: 9783337301934

Printed in Europe, USA, Canada, Australia, Japan

Cover: Foto ©Lupo / pixelio.de

More available books at **www.hansebooks.com**

OF THE

PROTESTANT EPISCOPAL CHURCH

IN THE

CONFEDERATE STATES OF AMERICA,

AND

DIGEST OF THE CANONS

ADOPTED IN

GENERAL COUNCIL, IN AUGUSTA, GEORGIA,

NOVEMBER, 1862.

TABLE OF CONTENTS.

...

TABLE OF CONTENTS.

————•·•————

.

DIGEST OF THE CANONS.

TITLE I.—Of Candidateship and Ordinations (*Continued.*)

TITLE II.—GENERAL REGULATIONS OF MINISTERS, &c. (Continued.)

CANON II.—General Regulations of Ministers (Continued)

TITLE III.—Of Discipline (Continued).

CANON VIII.—Of the Trial of a Bishop (Continued.)

CONSTITUTION.

CONSTITUTION.

ARTICLE I. This Church, retaining the name "Protestant Episcopal," shall be known as the "PROTESTANT EPISCOPAL CHURCH IN THE CONFEDERATE STATES OF AMERICA." _{Name.}

ARTICLE II. There shall be in this Church a General Council. There may be also Provincial Councils and Diocesan Councils. _{Councils.}

ARTICLE III. The General Council of this Church shall meet on the second Wednesday in November, in the year of our Lord one thousand eight hundred and sixty-two, at Augusta, Georgia, and on the same day in every third year thereafter, at such place as shall be determined by the Council. _{General Council.}

In case there shall be an epidemic disease, or other good cause to render it necessary to alter the place appointed for such meeting, the Presiding Bishop may designate another convenient place for the holding of such Council, and special meetings may be called at other times, in the manner hereafter to be determined.

The General Council shall consist of two Houses—the House of Bishops and the House of Deputies.

The House of Bishops shall be composed of all the Bishops of this Church having jurisdiction within the Confederate States, or the Territories thereof.

Each Diocese shall be entitled to an equal representation, clerical and lay, in the House of Deputies. Such representation shall consist of not more than three Clergymen, and three Laymen communicants in this Church, resident in the Diocese, and elected by the Council thereof.

Before they shall proceed to business, a majority of the Dioceses, which shall have adopted this Constitution, shall be represented in the Council. The representations from two Dioceses shall be sufficient to adjourn.

In all business of the Council freedom of debate shall be allowed.

2

Each House shall have a right to originate acts; and, when any act shall have been passed in either House, it shall be transmitted to the other House for its consideration. No act shall have the operation of law, unless concurred in and authenticated by both Houses.

When any proposed act shall have passed the House of Deputies, and shall be negatived by the House of Bishops, the House of Bishops shall, when requested by the House of Deputies, signify to it in writing the reasons for non-concurrence, within three days after such request shall have been made.

In all questions, when required by the clerical or lay representation from any Diocese, each order shall have one vote, and the majority of suffrages by Dioceses shall be conclusive in each order: *Provided* such majority comprehend a majority of the Dioceses represented in that order. The concurrence of both orders shall be necessary in such case to constitute a vote of the House.

.If any Diocese should omit or decline to elect clerical Deputies to the General Council, or should omit or decline to elect lay Deputies, or if any of those of either order elected should fail to attend, such Diocese shall, nevertheless, be considered as duly represented by such Deputy or Deputies as may attend, whether lay or clerical. And if, through the neglect of any Diocese, which shall have adopted this Constitution, no Deputy therefrom, either lay or clerical, should attend the Council, the Church in such Diocese shall, nevertheless, be bound by the acts of such Council.

Province.

ARTICLE IV. Whenever any one of the Confederate States shall contain more than one Diocese, said State may, with the consent of all the Dioceses in said State, constitute an Ecclesiastical Province, in which a Provincial
Provincial Council.
Council may be held at least once in every three years, which Provincial Council shall be made up of all the Bishops having jurisdiction within the Province, and of such representatives, clerical and lay, from the Dioceses within the Province, as may be determined upon by the Diocesan Councils thereof. If there be more than one Bishop within the Province, the senior Bishop by consecration shall preside in the Provincial Council, and when there shall be three, or more than three Bishops, they shall form a separate House.

Whenever such Council shall legislate, its acts shall be of force within all the Dioceses embraced within the Province.

ARTICLE V. There shall be held annually, in each Diocese, a Diocesan Council, to be composed of the Bishop or Bishops of the Diocese, and of a lay and clerical representation from each Parish of the Diocese. This Council shall legislate for only Diocesan purposes

ARTICLE VI. The Bishop or Bishops in each Diocese shall be chosen by the Council of that Diocese, agreeably to such rules as it may prescribe ; and every Bishop of this Church shall confine the exercise of his Episcopal Office to his proper Diocese, unless requested to perform any act of that Office by the Ecclesiastical Authority of another Diocese.

ARTICLE VII. A new Diocese, formed in any of the Confederate States, or in any Territory thereof, not now represented, may, at any time hereafter, be admitted to union with, and representation in, the General Council of this Church, on acceding to this. Constitution : *Provided* there were, at the time of organizing, and are, at the time of making application for admission, at least six officiating Presbyters within such Diocese, regularly settled in a Parish or Church.

A new Diocese may be formed within the limits of any existing Diocese, with the consent of its Council and the Bishop or Bishops thereof, or, if there be no Bishop, of the Ecclesiastical Authority thereof ; and a new Diocese may be formed within the limits of two or more Dioceses, with the like consent. But no such new Diocese shall be formed, which shall contain less than ten self-supporting Parishes, or less than ten Presbyters who have been for at least one year canonically resident within the bounds of such new Diocese, regularly settled in a Parish or Congregation, and qualified to vote for a Bishop; nor shall such new Diocese be formed if thereby any existing Diocese shall be so reduced as to contain less than fifteen self-supporting Parishes, or less than fifteen Presbyters who have been residing therein, and settled and qualified as above-mentioned : *Provided*, that no city shall form more than one Diocese.

In case a Diocese shall be divided into two or more Dioceses, the Diocesan of the Diocese so divided may elect the Diocese over which he will preside, and shall become the Diocesan thereof. And the Assistant Bishop, if there be one, may elect the Diocese to which he will be attached ; and, if it be not the one elected by the Bishop, he shall be the Diocesan thereof.

ARTICLE. VIII. The mode of trying Bishops shall be provided by the General Council. The court appointed for that purpose shall be composed of Bishops only.

In every Diocese, the mode of trying Presbyters and Deacons shall be prescribed by the Council of the Diocese.

None but a Bishop shall pronounce sentence of admonition, suspension or degradation from the ministry, on any Clergyman, whether Bishop, Presbyter or Deacon.

ARTICLE. IX. No person shall be admitted to Holy Orders, until he shall have been examined by the Bishop and by two Presbyters, and shall have exhibited such testimonials and other requisites as the Canons in that case provided may direct.

Nor shall any person be ordained either Deacon or Priest, until he shall have subscribed the following declaration, viz:

"I do believe the Holy Scriptures of the Old and New Testament to be the Word of God, and to contain all things necessary to salvation; and I do solemnly engage to conform to the Doctrines and Worship of the Protestant Episcopal Church in the Confederate States of America."

No person ordained by a foreign Bishop shall be permitted to officiate as a Minister of this Church, until he shall have complied with the Canon or Canons in such case provided, and have also subscribed the aforesaid declaration.

ARTICLE X. A Book of Common Prayer, Administration of the Sacraments and other Rites and Ceremonies of the Church, Articles of Religion, and a form and manner of making, ordaining and consecrating Bishops, Priests and Deacons, when established by the General Council, shall be used in those Dioceses which shall have adopted this Constitution. No alteration or addition shall be made in the Book of Common Prayer, or other offices of the Church, or the Articles of Religion, unless the same shall be proposed in one General Council, and by a resolution thereof made known to the Council of every Diocese, approved by a majority of the Diocesan Councils, and adopted at the subsequent General Council.

ARTICLE XI. Bishops for foreign countries may, on due application therefrom, be consecrated, with the approbation of a majority of the Bishops of this Church, signified in writing to the Presiding Bishop; he thereupon taking order for the same, and they being satisfied that the person designated for the office has been duly chosen and is properly qualified.

The order for such Consecration shall be conformed, as nearly as may be, in the judgment of the Bishops, to the one used in this Church.

Bishops, so consecrated, shall not be eligible to the office of Diocesan, or Assistant Bishop, in any Diocese in the Confederate States, nor be entitled to a seat in the House of Bishops, nor exercise any authority in the said States.

ARTICLE XII. Any alteration in this Constitution shall be originated in the General Council. When adopted in one General Council by a majority of the House of Bishops, and by a majority of the House of Deputies, said Deputies voting by Dioceses and orders, such alteration shall be made known to the several Diocesan Councils, and, if agreed to by two-thirds of them, and ratified in the ensuing General Council, the same shall be a part of this Constitution.

DIGEST OF THE CANONS.

TITLE I.

OF CANDIDATESHIP AND ORDINATIONS.

...

CANON I.

OF THE ECCLESIASTICAL AUTHORITY.

The Ecclesiastical Authority of each Diocese is its Bishop. When there is no Bishop, the Standing Committee shall be the Ecclesiastical Authority for all purposes declared in these Canons.

Ecclesiastical Authority.

...

CANON II.

OF THE ADMISSION OF PERSONS AS CANDIDATES FOR DEACONS' ORDERS.

§ 1. Every person, who desires to become a candidate for Holy Orders in this Church, shall, in the first instance, give notice in writing of that desire to the Ecclesiastical Authority to whose jurisdiction he belongs; in which notice he shall declare whether he has ever applied for admission as a candidate in any other Diocese. The Ecclesiastical Authority may consent to his applying in some other Diocese.

Notice of intention.

§ 2. The notice above required having been given to the Bishop, if there be one, and the Bishop having signified his approbation in writing, the person so applying shall send the said certificate in a letter addressed by him to the President or Secretary of the Standing Committee of the Diocese of the said Bishop; whereupon the Standing Committee may, if they see fit, testify in his behalf to the Bishop, that, from personal knowledge, or from testimonials laid before them, they believe that he is pious, sober and honest, attached to the doctrine, discipline and worship of the

Certificate.

2*

Protestant Episcopal Church, a communicant of the same, and in their opinion possesses such qualifications as will render him apt and meet to exercise the ministry to the glory of God, and the edifying of the Church; and if the Standing Committee cannot certify as above from personal knowledge, the testimonials laid before them by the applicant shall be of the same purport, and as full, as the certificate above required, and shall be signed by at least one Presbyter and four respectable laymen of the Protestant Episcopal Church in the Confederate States.

Admission and Record.

§ 3. The applicant shall transmit the certificate of the Standing Committee to the Bishop, who may thereupon admit the person as a candidate for Holy Orders, and shall record the same in a book to be kept by him for that purpose, and shall notify the candidate of such record. In any Diocese where there is no Bishop, the Standing Committee may, on the same conditions, admit the person as a candidate, and shall make record and notification in the same manner.

Refusal to Admit.

§ 4. No person who has previously applied for admission as a candidate in any Diocese, and has been refused, or, having been admitted, has afterwards ceased to be a candidate, shall be admitted as a candidate in any other Diocese, until he shall have produced from the Ecclesiastical Authority of the former Diocese a certificate declaring the cause for which he was refused admission, or for which he ceased to be a candidate.

Application by a Minister of any denomination.

§ 5. [1.] When a person, who, not having had Episcopal Ordination, has been acknowledged as an ordained minister or licentiate in any denomination of Christians, shall desire

Notice.

to be ordained in this Church, he shall give notice thereof to the Ecclesiastical Authority of the Diocese in which he resides; or, if he reside in a State or Territory in which there is no organized Diocese, to the Missionary Bishop within whose jurisdiction he resides; which notice shall be

Certificate.

accompanied by a written certificate from at least two Presbyters of this Church, stating that, from personal knowledge of the applicant, or satisfactory evidence laid before them, they believe that his desire to leave the denomination to which he belonged has not arisen from any circumstance unfavorable to his moral or religious character, or on account of which it may be inexpedient to admit him to the exercise of the ministry in this Church; and they may also add what they know or believe, on good authority, of the circumstances leading to the said desire.

TITLE I.—OF CANDIDATESHIP AND ORDINATIONS.

11

[2.] If the Ecclesiastical Authority shall think proper to proceed, the person applying to be received as a candidate shall produce to the Standing Committee a testimonial from at least twelve members of the denomination from which he comes, or twelve members of the Protestant Episcopal Church, or twelve persons in part of the denomination from which he comes and in part Episcopalians, satisfactory to the Committee, that the applicant has, for three years last past, lived piously, soberly and honestly; and also a testimonial from at least two Presbyters of this Church, that they believe him to be pious, sober and honest, and sincerely attached to the doctrine, discipline and worship of the Church. The Standing Committee, being satisfied on these points, may recommend him to the Bishop, to be received as a candidate for Orders in this Church; or, if there be no Bishop, the Standing Committee may so receive him.

§ 6. [1.] When a person, not a citizen of the Confederate States, who has been acknowledged as an ordained minister in any denomination of Christians, shall apply to become a candidate for Orders in this Church, the Bishop to whom application is made shall require of him (in addition to the above qualifications) satisfactory evidence that he has resided at least one year in the Confederate States, previous to his application.

[2.] When a person, not a citizen of the Confederate States, who has been acknowledged as an ordained minister in any denomination of Christians, shall apply for Orders in this Church on the ground of a call to a Church in which divine service is celebrated in a foreign language, the Standing Committee of the Diocese to which such Church belongs, may, on sufficient evidence of fitness according to the Canons, and by a unanimous vote at a meeting duly convened, recommend him to the Bishop for Orders, and the Bishop may then ordain him, and he may be settled, and instituted into the said Church, without his producing a testimonial to his character by a clergyman from his personal knowledge of him for one year, and without his having been a year resident in this country, anything in any other Canon of this Church to the contrary notwithstanding: *Provided*, That, in both of the above cases, the person applying produce a certificate, signed by at least four respectable members of this Church, that they have satisfactory reasons to believe the testimonials to his religious, moral and literary qualifications to be entitled to full credit.

CANON III.

OF ADMITTED CANDIDATES FOR DEACONS' ORDERS.

§ 1. The Bishop, or other Ecclesiastical Authority who may have the superintendence of candidates for Deacons' Orders, shall take care that they pursue their studies diligently and under proper direction, and that they do not indulge in any vain or trifling conduct, or in any amusements likely to be abused to licentiousness, or unfavorable to that seriousness, and to those pious and studious habits, which become those who are preparing for the Holy Ministry.

Supervision of Candidates.

§ 2. It is also to be made known to every candidate, that the Church expects of him, an inward fear and worship of Almighty God, a love of Christ, a sensibility to holy influences, a habit of devout affection, and, in short, a cultivation of all those graces which are called in Scripture, the fruits of the Spirit, by which alone His sacred influences can be manifested.

Habit of devotion.

§ 3. No candidate for Deacons' Orders shall take upon himself to perform the service of the Church but by a license from the Bishop, or, if there be no Bishop, from the clerical members of the Standing Committee, of the Diocese in which such candidate may wish to perform the service. And such candidate shall submit to all the regulations which the Bishop, or said clerical members, may prescribe. He shall not use the absolution or benediction; he shall not assume the dress appropriate to clergymen ministering in the congregation; he shall conform to the directions of the Bishop, or said clerical members, as to the sermons or homilies to be read; nor shall any such Lay Reader deliver sermons of his own composition, but, may make addresses or exhortations by the permission of the Bishop of the Diocese, and by the further permission of the Minister of the Parish, if within the limits of a Parish.

Lay Readers.

Restrictions.

§ 4. No candidate for Orders shall be permitted to accept from any Diocesan Council an appointment as a Lay Deputy to the House of Deputies of the General Council.

Not eligible to General Council.

§ 5. A candidate for Deacons' Orders may, on Letters Dimissory from the Ecclesiastical Authority of the Diocese to which he belongs, be transferred to the jurisdiction of any Bishop in this Church; and if there be a Bishop of the Diocese where the candidate resides, he shall apply to no

Transfer to other Dioceses.

other Bishop for ordination without the permission of the former.

§ 6. No candidate shall change his canonical residence but for causes sufficient in the judgment of the Ecclesiastical Authority; nor shall any candidate be dismissed from the Diocese in which he was admitted, or to which he has been duly transferred, for the convenience of attending any theological or other seminary.

•••

CANON IV.

GENERAL PROVISIONS AND REQUISITES FOR ORDINATION.

§ 1. No Bishop shall ordain any candidate until he has enquired of him whether he has ever, directly or indirectly, applied for Holy Orders in any other Diocese ; and, if the Bishop has reason to believe that the candidate has been refused Holy Orders in any other Diocese, he shall write to the Ecclesiastical Authority thereof to know whether any just cause exists why the candidate should not be ordained. When any Bishop rejects an application for Holy Orders, he shall immediately give notice to the Ecclesiastical Authority of every Diocese.

§ 2. Deacons' Orders shall not be conferred on any person until he shall be twenty-one years old. nor Priests' Orders until he shall be twenty-four years old.

§ 3. Every candidate for Holy Orders who may be recommended by the Standing Committee of any Diocese destitute of a Bishop, if he have resided for the greater part of three years last past within the Diocese of a Bishop, shall apply to such Bishop for ordination. And such candidate shall produce the usual testimonials, as well from the Committee of the Diocese in which he has resided, as from the Committee of the Diocese for which he is to be ordained.

§ 4. No Bishop of this Church shall ordain any person to officiate as a Priest in any Congregation or Church not under Episcopal supervision, and situated beyond the jurisdiction of these Confederate States, until he shall have received from his Standing Committee the usual testimony, founded upon sufficient evidence of the soundness in the faith, and of the pious and moral character of the applicant.

nor until he has been examined on the studies prescribed by the Canons of this Church; and should any clergyman, so ordained, wish thereafter to settle in any congregation of this Church, he must obtain a special license therefor from the Bishop, and officiate as a probationer for at least one year.

Times of Ordination. § 5. Agreeably to the practice of the Primitive Church, the stated times of ordination shall be on the Sundays following the Ember weeks. Special ordinations may be held at such other times as the Bishop shall appoint.

...

CANON V.

EXAMINATIONS AND TESTIMONIALS FOR DEACONS' ORDERS AND ORDINATION.

Examination. § 1. Every person hereafter to be ordained Deacon in this Church, shall be examined by the Bishop and two Presbyters, on Moral Philosophy and Rhetoric, the Holy Scriptures and the Book of Common Prayer, and they shall enquire into his fitness for the ministrations declared in the Ordinal to appertain to the office of a Deacon. and be satisfied thereof.

Limitation of Candidateship. §.2. If any candidate for Deacons' Orders shall not, within three years after his admission, apply to be ordained, he shall cease to be a candidate. and unless the Bishop shall see fit to allow longer time, he shall notify him in writing, that he is no longer a candidate, and shall immediately give notice of the same to the Ecclesiastical Authority of every Diocese.

Period of Candidateship and Testimonials from Standing Committee. § 3. No person shall be ordained Deacon in this Church until he shall have remained a candidate for Holy Orders at least one year, and until he shall exhibit to the Bishop testimonials from the Standing Committee of the Diocese for which he is to be ordained, which shall be signed by a majority of all the Committee. the Committee being duly convened, and which shall be in the following words:

" We, whose names are hereunder written, testify that A. B. hath laid before us satisfactory testimonials. that for the space of three years last past, he hath lived piously, soberly and honestly, and hath not written. taught or held anything contrary to the doctrine or discipline of the Protestant Episcopal Church in the Confederate States; and, moreover,. we think him a person worthy to be admitted to the sacred Order of Deacons. In witness whereof, we have hereunto set our hands. this ———— day of ———, in the year of our Lord ———."

§ 4. But before a Standing Committee shall proceed to recommend any candidate, as aforesaid, to the Bishop, such candidate shall produce from the Minister and Vestry of the parish where he resides, or from the Vestry alone, if the parish be vacant; or, if there be no Vestry, from at least six respectable persons of this Church, testimonials of his piety, good morals and orderly conduct, in the following words:

"We, whose names are hereunder written, do testify from evidence satisfactory to us, that A. B., for the space of three years last past, hath lived piously, soberly and honestly, and hath not, so far as we know or believe, written, taught or held anything contrary to the doctrine or discipline of the Protestant Episcopal Church in the Confederate States; and, moreover, we think him a person worthy to be admitted to the sacred Order of Deacons. In witness whereof, we have hereunto set our hands, this ——— day of ———, in the year of our Lord ———."

He shall also lay before the Standing Committee testimonials signed by at least one respectable Presbyter of this Church, which testimonials shall be in the following words:

"I do certify that A. B., for the space of three years last past, hath lived piously, soberly and honestly, and hath not, so far as I know or believe, written, taught or held anything contrary to the doctrine or discipline of the Protestant Episcopal Church in the Confederate States; and, moreover, we think him a person worthy to be admitted to the sacred Order of Deacons. This testimonial is founded on my personal knowledge of the said A. B. for one year last past, and for the residue of the said time upon evidence that is satisfactory to me. In witness whereof, I have hereunto set my hand, this ——— day of ———, in the year of our Lord ———."

§ 5. But in case a candidate, from some peculiar circumstances not affecting his pious or moral character, shall be unable to procure testimonials from the Minister and Vestry of the Parish wherein he resides, the Standing Committee may accept testimonials of the purport above stated, from at least twelve respectable members, and one respectable Presbyter of this Church, which Presbyter shall have been personally acquainted with the candidate for at least one year.

§ 6. Candidates who, not having Episcopal ordination, have been acknowledged as ordained or licensed ministers in any denomination of Christians, may, at the expiration of not less than six months from their admission as candidates, be ordained Deacons, on their passing the same examinations as other candidates for Deacons' Orders, and, in the examinations, special regard shall be had to those points in which the denomination whence they came differs from this Church, with a view of testing their information

Canon V.

and soundness in the same ; and, also, of ascertaining that they are adequately acquainted with the Liturgy and Offices of this Church : *Provided*, that in their case the testimonials shall be required to cover only the time since their admission as candidates for Holy Orders.

Candinates from other countries.

§ 7. When any person, not a citizen of the Confederate States, who has been acknowledged as an ordained or licensed minister in any denomination of Christians, shall apply for Orders in this Church, the Bishop, to whom the application is made, shall require of him (in addition to the above qualifications) satisfactory evidence that he has resided at least one year in the Confederate States previous to his application.

CANON VI.

OF DEACONS.

Control of Deacons.

§ 1. Every Deacon shall be subject to the regulation of the Bishop, or, if there be no Bishop, of the clerical members of the Standing Committee of the Diocese for which he is ordained, until he receive letters dimissory to the Ecclesiastical Authority of some other Diocese, and be thereupon received as a Clergyman of such other Diocese : and he shall officiate in such places as the Bishop, or the said clerical members, may direct.

Conditions of officiating.

§ 2. No Deacon shall be settled over a Parish or Congregation ; nor shall any Deacon officiate in any Parish or Congregation, without the express consent of the Rector for the time being, where there is a Rector ; nor in any case without the assent of the Bishop ; and when officiating in the Parish or Congregation of a Rector, he shall be entirely subject to the direction of such Rector in all his ministrations.

Transfer.

§ 3. No Deacon shall be transferred to another Diocese without the written request of the Bishop. to whose jurisdiction he is to be transferred.

CANON VII.

ORDINATION TO THE PRIESTHOOD.

Deacon proceeding to Priests' Orders.

§ 1. Whenever a Deacon shall determine to proceed to Priests' Orders. he shall give to the Bishop written notice of such intention ; whereupon the Bishop shall record the notice in a book to be kept by him for this purpose, and shall appoint and direct the studies of the Deacon accordingly.

§ 2. Every Deacon desiring to receive Priests' Orders shall stand three different examinations, at such times and places as the Bishop, to whom he applies for Holy Orders, shall appoint. The examination shall take place in the presence of the Bishop and two or more Presbyters. The first examination shall be on the books of Scripture, the candidate being required to give an account of the different books, to translate from the original Greek and Hebrew, and to explain such passages as may be proposed to him. The second examination shall be on the evidences of Christianity and Systematic Divinity, and the last examination shall be on Church History, Ecclesiastical Polity, the Book of Common Prayer, and the Constitution and Canons of the Church, and of the Diocese for which he is to be ordained. He shall be examined also as to his knowledge of the Latin tongue, and of such studies as the Bishop shall have prescribed for him. At each of the forementioned examinations he shall produce and read a sermon or discourse, composed by himself, on some passage of Scripture, previously assigned to him, which, together with two other sermons or discourses on some passage or passages of Scripture selected by himself, shall be submitted to the criticisms of the Bishop and clergy present ; and, before his ordination, he shall be required to perform such exercises in reading, in the presence of the Bishop and clergy, as may enable them to give him such advice and instructions as may aid him in performing the services of the Church, and delivering his sermons with propriety and devotion.

§ 3. When a Deacon, applying to be admitted to Priests' Orders, wishes knowledge of the Latin, Greek and Hebrew languages, and other branches of learning not strictly ecclesiastical, to be dispensed with, the Standing Committee shall not recommend him for Priests' Orders until he shall have laid before them a testimonial signed by at least two Presbyters of this Church, stating that, in their opinion, he possesses a peculiar aptitude to teach, and a large share of prudence ; and the Bishop, with the consent of the Standing Committee, shall have granted the dispensation. But in regard to a knowledge of the Hebrew language, the Bishop shall have the sole power of dispensation.

3

Canon VII.

Where there is
no Bishop.

§ 4. In a Diocese where there is no Bishop, the Deacon shall be examined by the Bishop to whom he applies for Holy Orders, and by two or more Presbyters appointed for that purpose by the said Bishop.

Testimonials
from Standing
Committee.

§ 5. No person shall be ordained a Priest in this Church until he shall have exhibited to the Bishop testimonials from the Standing Committee of the Diocese for which he is to be ordained, which testimonials shall be signed with the names of a majority of all the Committee, the Committee being duly convened, and shall be in the following words:

"We, whose names are underwritten, members of the Standing Committee of the Diocese of —————, do testify that the Rev. A. B., Deacon, hath laid before us satisfactory testimonials, that for the space of three years last past, he hath lived piously, soberly and honestly, and hath not written, taught or held anything contrary to the doctrine or discipline of the Protestant Episcopal Church in the Confederate States; and, moreover, we think him a person worthy to be admitted to the sacred Order of Priests. In witness whereof, we have hereunto set our hands this ————— day of ————, in the year of our Lord —————."

Testimonials to
Standing Committee.

But before the Standing Committee shall proceed to recommend any Deacon, as aforesaid, to the Bishop, such Deacon shall produce from the Minister and Vestry of the Parish where he resides, or, if the Parish be vacant, from the Vestry alone, testimonials of his piety, good morals and orderly conduct, in the following words:

"We, whose names are hereunder written, do testify that the Rev. A. B., Deacon, hath, for the space of three years last past, lived piously, soberly and honestly, and hath not, so far as we know or believe, written, taught or held anything contrary to the doctrine or discipline of the Protestant Episcopal Church in the Confederate States; and, moreover, we think him a person worthy to be admitted to the sacred Order of Priests. In witness whereof, we have hereunto set our hands this ————— day of ————, in the year of our Lord —————."

Testimonials of
a Presbyter.

He shall also lay before the Standing Committee testimonials signed by at least one respectable Presbyter of this Church, in the following form:

"I do certify, that the Rev. A. B., Deacon, has, for the space of three years last past, lived piously, soberly and honestly, and has not, so far as I know or believe, written, taught or held anything contrary to the doctrine or discipline of the Protestant Episcopal Church in the Confederate States; and, moreover, I think him a person worthy to be admitted to the sacred Order of Priests. This testimonial is founded on my personal knowledge of the said Rev. A. B., Deacon, for one year last past, and for the residue of the said time upon evidence that is satisfactory to me. In witness whereof, I have hereunto set my hand this ————— day of ————, in the year of our Lord —————."

Substitute testimonials.

§ 6. But in case an applicant for Priests' Orders shall, from peculiar circumstances, not affecting his pious or moral character, be unable to procure testimonials from the Minister and Vestry of the Parish where he resides, or in case of there being no Vestry, the Standing Committee may accept testimonials of the purport above stated from at least twelve respectable members, and from at least one respectable Presbyter of this Church, who has been personally acquainted with the candidate for at least one year.

...

CANON VIII.

OF THE ADMISSION OF MINISTERS ORDAINED BY BISHOPS NOT IN COMMUNION WITH THIS CHURCH.

When a Deacon or Priest, ordained by a Bishop not in communion with this Church, shall apply to a Bishop for admission into the same as a minister thereof, he shall produce a written certificate from at least two Presbyters of this Church, stating that, from personal knowledge of him, or satisfactory evidence laid before them, they believe that his desire to leave the communion to which he has belonged has not arisen from any circumstance unfavorable to his moral or religious character, or on account of which it may be inexpedient to admit him to the exercise of the ministry in this Church; and he shall also, not less than six months after his application, in the presence of the Bishop and two or more Presbyters, subscribe the declaration contained in Article IX. of the Constitution; which being done, the Bishop, being satisfied of his theological acquirements, may receive him as such minister.

Ministers ordained by Bishops not in communion with this Church.

...

CANON IX.

OF MINISTERS ORDAINED IN FOREIGN COUNTRIES BY BISHOPS IN COMMUNION WITH THIS CHURCH.

§ 1. A clergyman coming from a foreign country, and professing to have been ordained out of the Confederate States by a foreign Bishop in communion with this Church, or by a Bishop consecrated for a foreign country by Bishops of this Church under Article XI. of the Constitution.

Ministers ordained in foreign countries by Bishops in communion with this Church.

or by a Missionary Bishop elected to exercise Episcopal functions in any place or places out of the Confederate States, shall, before he be permitted to officiate in any Parish or Congregation, exhibit to the Minister, or, if there be no Minister, to the Vestry thereof, a certificate signed by the Bishop of the Diocese, or, if there be no Bishop, by the Standing Committee duly convened, that his letters of Holy Orders are authentic, and given by some Bishop in communion with this Church, and whose authority is acknowledged by this Church; and, also, 'that he has exhibited to the Bishop or Standing Committee satisfactory evidence of his pious and moral character, and of his theological acquirements; and, in any case, before he shall be permitted to settle in any Church or Parish, or be received into union with any Diocese of this Church as a minister thereof, he shall produce to the Ecclesiastical Authority thereof, letters dimissory under the hand and seal of the Bishop with whose Diocese he has been last connected which letters shall be, in substance, those provided for in Section 7 of Canon II. of Title II., and shall be delivered within six months from the date thereof; and when such clergyman shall have been so received, he shall be considered as having passed entirely from the jurisdiction of the Bishop from whom the letters dimissory were brought, to the full jurisdiction of the Ecclesiastical Authority by whom they shall have been accepted, and become thereby subject to all the canonical provisions of this Church : *Provided*, that no such clergyman shall be so received into union with any Diocese until he shall have subscribed, in the presence of the Bishop of the Diocese in which he applies for reception, and of two or more Presbyters, the declaration contained in Article IX. of the Constitution; which being done, said Bishop or Standing Committee, being satisfied of his theological acquirements, may receive him into union with this Church as a minister of the same : *Provided, also,* that such minister shall not be entitled to settle in any Parish or Church, as canonically in charge of the same, until he shall, subsequently to the acceptance of his letters dimissory, have resided one year in the Confederate States.

§ 2. And if such foreign clergyman be a Deacon, he shall obtain in this country the requisite testimonials of character, before he be ordained a Priest.

TITLE II.
GENERAL REGULATIONS OF MINISTERS AND THEIR DUTIES.

--- •••----

CANON I.
THE CONSENT NECESSARY FOR OFFICIATING.

No Minister shall officiate, transiently or otherwise, in a Congregation or vacant Parish, or in one the Rector or Minister of which is sick or absent, unless the Wardens, Vestry or Trustees of the Congregation are satisfied that he is at the time an Episcopally ordained Minister in good and regular standing. When from another Diocese, letters commendatory from the Ecclesiastical Authority thereof may be required.

In case of Ministers.

--- •••• -

CANON II.
GENERAL REGULATIONS OF MINISTERS.

§ 1. [1.] It is hereby required that, on the election of a Minister into any Church or Parish, the Vestry shall deliver, or cause to be delivered, to the Ecclesiastical Authority of the Diocese, notice of the same, in the following form :

Election of Ministers.

"We, the Church Wardens, (*or, in case of an Assistant Minister*, we, the Rector and Church Wardens) do certify to the Rt. Rev'd, (*naming the Bishop*) or to the Rev'd, (*naming the President of the Standing Committee*) that (*naming the person*) has been duly chosen Rector (or assistant Minister, *as the case may be*,) of (*naming the Parish or Church*.)"

Certificate of election.

Which certificate shall be signed with the names of those who certify.

Canon II.

To be recorded.

[2.] If the Ecclesiastical Authority be satisfied that the person so chosen is a qualified Minister of this Church, the said Ecclesiastical Authority shall transmit the said certificate to the Secretary of the Council, who shall record it in a book to be kept by him for that purpose.

Institution.

[3.] And if the Minister be a Presbyter, the Ecclesiastical Authority may, at the instance of the Vestry, proceed to have him instituted according to the Office established by this Church, if that Office be used in the Diocese. This provision, concerning the use of the Office of Institution, is not to be considered as applying to any Congregation destitute of a house of worship.

Certificate to Minister removing from one Diocese to another.

§ 2. No Minister, removing from one Diocese or Missionary District to another, shall officiate as the Rector, Stated Minister, or Assistant Minister of any Parish or Congregation of the Diocese or District to which he removes, until he shall have obtained from the Ecclesiastical Authority a certificate in the words following:

"I hereby certify that the Rev. A. B. has been canonically transferred to my jurisdiction, and is a Minister in regular standing."

Alms at Communion.

§ 3. The Alms and Contributions at the administration of the Holy Communion shall be deposited with the Minister of the Parish, or with such Church officer as shall be appointed by him, to be applied by the Minister, or under his superintendence, to such pious and charitable uses as shall by him be thought fit.

Duty of Ministers about Confirmations.

§ 4. [1.] It shall be the duty of Ministers to prepare young persons and others for the holy ordinance of Confirmation. And on notice being received from the Bishop of his intention to visit any Church for the purpose of administering that rite, which notice shall be at least one month before the intended visitation, the Minister shall give immediate notice to his parishioners, individually, as opportunity may offer, and also to the Congregation on the first occasion of public worship after the receipt of said notice. And he shall be ready to present for confirmation such persons as he shall think properly qualified, and shall deliver to the Bishop a list of the names of those confirmed.

About the state of the Congregation.

[2.] And at every visitation the Minister and Church Wardens, or Vestry, shall lay before the Bishop, if required, the Parish records, and give information to him of the state of the Congregation, under such heads as shall have been committed to them in the notice given as aforesaid.

For the Diocesan Council.

[3.] And further, the Ministers and Church Wardens of such Congregations as cannot be conveniently visited in any year, shall bring or send to the Bishop, at the stated meeting of the Council of the Diocese, information of the state of the Congregation, under such heads as shall have been committed to them at least one month before the meeting of the Council.

§ 5. [1.] Every Minister of this Church shall keep a register of baptisms, confirmations, communicants, marriages and funerals, within his cure, agreeably to such rules as may be provided by the Council of the Diocese where his cure lies; and if none such be provided, then in such manner as in his discretion he shall think best suited to the uses of such a register.

[2.] The intention of the Register of Baptisms is hereby declared to be, as for other good uses, so especially for the proving of the right of the Church-membership of those who may have been admitted into this Church by the holy ordinance of Baptism.

[3.] Every Minister of this Church shall make out and continue, as far as practicable, a list of all families and adult persons within his cure, which, with all other Parish records in his keeping, shall, in case of his removal, be entrusted to the Wardens of the Church, to remain for the use of his successor, to be continued by him and by every future Minister in the same Parish.

§ 6. [1.] No Minister belonging to this Church shall officiate, either by preaching, reading prayers or otherwise, in the Parish, or within the parochial cure of another clergyman, without the consent of the Minister of the Parish or cure, or, in his absence, of the Church Wardens and Vestrymen, or Trustees of the Congregation, or a majority of them.

[2.] If any Minister of this Church, from inability or other cause, fail to perform the regular services in his Congregation, and refuse, without good cause, his consent to the officiating of any other Minister of this Church within his cure, the Church Wardens, Vestrymen or Trustees of such Congregation shall, on proof of such failure or refusal before the Ecclesiastical Authority, or before such persons as may be deputed thereby, or before such persons as may be, by the regulations of this Church in any Diocese, vested with the power of hearing and deciding on complaints against Clergymen, have power, with the written consent of the beforementioned authority, to open the doors of their Church to any regular Minister of this Church.

§ 7. [1.] A Minister of this Church removing within the jurisdiction of any Bishop or other Ecclesiastical Authority.

Marginal notes:
Canon II.

Parish Register.

To prove Church membership.

List of families.

Officiating of Ministers in the cures of others.

Neglect of Ministers.

Clerical residence.

shall, in order to gain canonical residence within the same, present to said Ecclesiastical Authority a testimonial from the Ecclesiastical Authority of the Diocese or Missionary District in which he last resided, which testimonial shall set forth his true standing and character. The testimonial may be in the following words:

Letters dimissory.
"I hereby certify that A. B., who has signified to me his desire to be transferred to the Ecclesiastical Authority of ———, is a Presbyter (or Deacon) of ———, in regular standing, and has not, so far as I know or believe, been justly liable to evil report, for error in religion or viciousness of life, for three years last past."

All such testimonials shall be called Letters Dimissory.

When to affect canonical residence.
[2.] No such letters shall affect a Minister's canonical residence, until, after having been presented according to address, they shall have been accepted, and notification of such acceptance given to the authority whence it proceeded. The residence of the Minister so transferred shall date from the acceptance of his letters dimissory. If not presented within three months after date, they may be considered as

When void.
void by the authority whence they proceeded; and shall be so considered, unless they be presented within six months.

Reception.
[3.] If a Minister, removing into another Diocese, who has been called to take charge of a Parish or Congregation, shall present a testimonial in the form aforesaid, it shall be the duty of the Ecclesiastical Authority of the Diocese to

When to be granted.
which he has removed, to accept it, unless the Bishop or Standing Committee should have heard rumors, which he or they believe to be well founded, against the character of the Minister concerned, and which would form a proper ground of canonical inquiry and presentment; in which case the Ecclesiastical Authority shall communicate the same to the Ecclesiastical Authority of the Diocese to whose juris-

When refused.
diction the said Minister belongs; and, in such case, it shall not be the duty of the Ecclesiastical Authority to accept the testimonial unless, and until there be satisfactory explanation of such rumors.

Letters dimissory, when not required.
[4.] It shall be the duty of all Ministers, except chaplains in the army and navy, and professors and officers in institutions under the direction of the General Council, to obtain and present letters dimissory as above described, whenever they remove from one Diocese or Missionary District to any other Diocese or Missionary District, whether Domestic or Foreign, and remain there for the space of six months. If, at the end of that time, any Minister, so removing, shall not have obtained and presented such letters, the Bishop or

the Diocese from which he has removed shall have the right to transfer him by letters dimissory into the Diocese of the Bishop into whose jurisdiction he has removed.

§ 8. A Minister is settled for all purposes here or elsewhere mentioned in these Canons, who has been engaged permanently by any Parish, according to the rules of the Diocese to which the Parish belongs, or for any term not less than one year.

Canon II.

---·•·---

CANON III.

OF BISHOPS.

§ 1. To entitle a Diocese to the choice of a Bishop by the Council thereof, there must be, at the time of such choice, and have been during the year previous, at least six officiating Presbyters therein, regularly settled in a Parish or Church, and qualified to vote for a Bishop, and six or more Parishes represented in the Council electing.

Election of Bishop.

§ 2. [1.] Whenever the Church in any Diocese shall be desirous of the consecration of a Bishop elect, the Standing Committee of the Church in such Diocese shall, by their President, or by some person or persons specially appointed, communicate the desire to the Standing Committees of the Churches in the different Dioceses, together with evidence of his election, and a certified copy of the following testimonial :

Process for consecration.

Testimony from the Members of the Council in the Diocese from whence the Person is recommended for Consecration.

Testimony from Diocesan Council.

" We, whose names are underwritten, fully sensible how important it is that the sacred office of a Bishop should not be unworthily conferred, and firmly persuaded that it is our duty to bear testimony on this solemn occasion, without partiality or affection, do, in the presence of Almighty God, testify that A. B. is not, so far as we are informed, justly liable to evil report, either for error in religion, or for viciousness in life, and that we do not know or believe there is any impediment, on account of which he ought not to be consecrated to that Holy Office. We do, moreover, jointly and severally, declare that we do, in our conscience, believe him to be of such sufficiency in good learning, such soundness in the faith, and of such virtues and pure manners, and godly conversation, that he is apt and meet to exercise the office of a Bishop to the honor of God, and the edifying of His Church, and to be a wholesome example to the flock of Christ."

[2.] The evidence of the consent of the Standing Committees shall be in the form following :

3*

Testimony from the Standing Committee of (naming the Diocese).

Canon III.

Testimony from the Standing Committee.

" We, whose names are underwritten, fully sensible how important it is that the sacred office of a Bishop should not be unworthily conferred, and firmly persuaded that it is our duty to bear testimony, on this solemn occasion, without partiality or affection, do, in the presence of Almighty God, testify that A. B. is not, so far as we are informed, justly liable to evil report, either for error in religion, or for viciousness of life; and that we do not know or believe there is any impediment, on account of which he ought not to be consecrated to that Holy Office, but that he hath, as we believe, led his life, for three years last past, piously, soberly and honestly."

Consent of Bishops.

[3.] And if the major number of the Standing Committees shall consent to the proposed consecration, the Standing Committee of the Diocese concerned shall forward the evidence of such consent, together with other testimonials, to the Senior Bishop of this Church, who shall communicate the same to all the Bishops of this Church in the Confederate States; and if a majority of the Bishops consent to the consecration, the Senior Bishop, with two other Bishops, or any three Bishops to whom he may communicate the testimonials, may proceed to perform the same.

Consecration of Bishops elected within three months of the meeting of the General Council.

[4.] When the election of a Bishop occurs within the three months preceding the regular meeting of the General Council, the Standing Committee of the Diocese shall communicate to the General Council the desire of the Diocese for the consecration of the Bishop elect, together with evidence of his election, and the testimonial required by § 2, [1.] of this Canon; and, if a majority of both Orders in the House of Deputies shall consent to the proposed consecration, and shall sign and transmit to the House of Bishops the testimony contained in § 2. [2.] of this Canon; and if a majority of the Bishops entitled to seats in the House of Bishops shall consent to the proposed consecration, the Presiding Bishop shall take order for the same.

Place of Consecration.

[5.] The consecration of a Bishop shall, if practicable, take place always in the Diocese of which he is the Bishop elect.

Age.

§ 3. No man shall be consecrated a Bishop of this Church until he shall be thirty years old.

Assistant Bishop.

§ 4. When a Bishop of a Diocese is unable, by reason of old age, or other permanent cause of infirmity, to discharge his Episcopal duties, one Assistant Bishop may be elected by and for the said Diocese, who shall, in all cases, succeed the Bishop, in case of surviving him. The Assistant Bishop shall perform such Episcopal duties, and exercise such Episcopal authority in the Diocese, as the Bishop shall assign to him; and, in case of the Bishop's inability to assign such duties, declared by the Council of the Diocese, the Assistant Bishop shall, during such inability, perform all the duties, and exercise all the authorities which appertain to the office of a Bishop. No person shall be elected or consecrated a Suffragan Bishop, nor shall there be more than one Assistant Bishop in a Diocese at the same time.

Canon III.

No Suffragans.

§ 5. [1.] Every Bishop of this Church shall visit the Churches within his Diocese at least once in three years, for the purpose of examining the state of his Church, inspecting the behaviour of his clergy, administering the apostolic rite of confirmation, ministering the Word, and if he think fit, administering the Sacrament of the Lord's Supper to the people committed to his charge, and shall keep a register of all his official acts.

Episcopal visitations.

[2.] No Bishop of this Church shall reside beyond the limits of his Diocese, unless with the consent of three fourths of his Diocesan Council given at each of its Sessions.

Episcopal residence.

§ 6. It shall be lawful for any Bishop of a Diocese, who is about to leave or has left his Diocese, with the intention of going out of the limits of the Confederate States, or if remaining out of his Diocese for the space of three calendar months, although without leaving the Confederate States, to authorize, by writing under his hand and seal, the Assistant Bishop, or, should there be none, the Standing Committee of such Diocese, to act as the Ecclesiastical Authority thereof. The Assistant Bishop, or Standing Committee so authorized, shall thereupon become the Ecclesiastical Authority of such Diocese, to all intents and purposes, until such writing shall be revoked, or the Bishop shall return within the Diocese: *Provided*, That nothing in this Canon shall be so construed as to prevent any Bishop, who may have signed such writing, from exercising his jurisdiction himself, so far as the same may be practicable, during his absence from his Diocese, or from permitting and authorizing any other Bishop to perform Episcopal offices for him.

Bishops absent for a time.

§ 7. The Bishop of each Diocese may compose forms of prayer or thanksgiving, as the case may require, for extraordinary occasions, and transmit them to each Clergyman within his Diocese, whose duty it shall be to use such forms in his Church on such occasions. And the Clergy in those States or Dioceses, or other places within the bounds of this Church, in which there is no Bishop, may use the form of prayer or thanksgiving composed by the Bishop of any Diocese. The Bishop in each Diocese may also compose forms of prayer to be used before legislative and other public bodies.

Forms of prayer and thanksgiving for extraordinary occasions.

§ 8. Any Bishop exercising jurisdiction, may, on the invitation of the Council or the Standing Committee of any Diocese where there is no Bishop, or where the Bishop is, for the time, under a disability to perform Episcopal Offices by reason of a judicial sentence, visit and perform Episcopal Offices in that Diocese, or in any part thereof; and this invitation may be temporary, and it may at any time be revoked.

§ 9. [1.] The House of Deputies may, from time to time, on nomination by the House of Bishops, elect a suitable person to be a Bishop of this Church, to exercise Episcopal functions in States or Territories not organized into Dioceses. The evidence of such election shall be a certificate, to be subscribed by a constitutional majority of said House of Deputies, in the form required by § 2. of this Canon to be given by the members of Diocesan Councils, on the recommendation of Bishops elect for consecration, which certificate shall be produced to the House of Bishops; and if the House of Bishops shall consent to the consecration, they may take order for that purpose.

[2.] The Bishop so elected and consecrated shall exercise Episcopal functions in such States and Territories, in conformity with the Constitution and Canons of this Church, and under such regulations and instructions, not inconsistent therewith, as the House of Bishops may prescribe; and the House of Bishops may at any time increase or diminish the number of States or Territories over which the said Bishop or Bishops shall exercise Episcopal functions.

[3.] In case of the death or resignation of a Missionary Bishop, or of vacancy by other cause, the charge of the vacant Missionary Episcopate shall, until another Bishop be elected and consecrated, devolve on the senior Bishop of this Church, with the power of appointing some other Bishop as his substitute in said charge.

[4.] Any Bishop elected and consecrated under this section, shall be eligible to the office of Diocesan Bishop in any organized Diocese within the Confederate States, with the consent of three-fourths of the Bishops having seats in the House of Bishops, and of the Standing Committees of three fourths of the several Dioceses, said consent to be signified to the Senior Bishop and announced by him; or, if the Missionary Bishop be elected Diocesan within three months preceding the meeting of the General Council, with the consent of three-fourths of both orders present in the House of Deputies, and of three-fourths of the Bishops present in the House of Bishops. And whenever a Diocese shall have been organized within the jurisdiction of such Missionary Bishop, if he shall be chosen Bishop of such Diocese, he may accept the office, and shall thereby vacate his missionary appointment: *Provided*, That he continue to discharge the duties of Missionary Bishop within the residue of his original jurisdiction, if there be such residue, until the meeting of the next General Council. Canon III.

[5.] Every such Bishop may yearly appoint two Presbyters, and two Laymen communicants of this Church, resident within his missionary jurisdiction, to perform the duties of a Standing Committee for such jurisdiction: *Provided*, That no Standing Committee constituted under this Section shall have power to give or refuse assent to the consecration of a Bishop. *May appoint Standing Committee.*

[6.] Every such Bishop shall report to each General Council his official acts, and the state and condition of the Church in said States and Territories of the Confederate States. *Report to General Council.*

§ 10. [1.] The House of Deputies may, from time to time, on nomination by the House of Bishops, elect a suitable person to be a Bishop of this Church, to exercise Episcopal functions in any missionary station of this Church out of the Territory of the Confederate States, which the House of Bishops, with the concurrence of the House of Deputies, may have designated. The evidence of such election shall be a certificate, to be subscribed by a constitutional majority of said House of Deputies, expressing their assent to the said nomination, which certificate shall be produced to the House of Bishops; and if the House of Bishops shall consent to the consecration, they may take order for that purpose. *Foreign Missionary Bishops.* *Evidence of election.*

[2.] Any Bishop elected and consecrated under this Section, or any foreign Missionary Bishop heretofore consecrated to exercise Episcopal functions in any place or country which may have been thus designated, shall have no jurisdiction, except in the place or country for which he has been elected and consecrated. He shall be entitled to a seat, but not a vote, in the House of Bishops. He shall not become a Diocesan Bishop in any organized Diocese within the Confederate States, unless with the consent of three-fourths of all the Bishops entitled to seats in the House of Bishops, and also with the consent of the Standing Committees of three-fourths of the Dioceses. *Jurisdiction.*

[3.] Any Bishop elected and consecrated under this Section, or any Foreign Missionary Bishop heretofore consecrated, may ordain as Deacons or Presbyters, to officiate *May ordain.*

within the limits of his Mission, any persons of the age required by the Canons of this Church, who shall exhibit to him the testimonials required by Canons V. and VII. of Title I., signed by not less than two of the ordained Missionaries of this Church who may be subject to his charge: *Provided, nevertheless*, That if there be only one ordained Missionary attached to the Mission, and capable of acting at the time, the signature of a Presbyter, under the jurisdiction of any Bishop in communion with this Church, in good standing, may be admitted to supply the deficiency.

[4.] Any Foreign Missionary Bishop consecrated under this Section, or heretofore consecrated, may, by and with the advice of two Presbyters, one of whom, if necessity require, shall be a Presbyter in good standing under the jurisdiction of any Bishop in communion with this Church, dispense with those studies required from a candidate for Orders by the Canons of this Church:

Provided, No person shall be ordained Priest by him, who has not passed a satisfactory examination, in the presence of two Presbyters, as to his theological learning and aptitude to teach: *And provided, further*, That no person shall be ordained Deacon by him, until he shall have been a candidate for at least one year.

Nor shall any Deacon or Priest, who shall have been ordained under this Section, be allowed to hold any cure, or officiate in the Church in these Confederate States, until he shall have complied with existing Canons, relating to the learning of persons to be ordained.

[5.] Any Foreign Missionary Bishop elected and consecrated under this Section, or any Foreign Missionary Bishop heretofore consecrated, shall have jurisdiction and government according to the Canons of this Church, over all Missionaries or Clergymen of this Church, resident in the district or country for which he may have been consecrated.

[6.] Every such Bishop may yearly appoint not less than two, nor more than five Presbyters, resident within his missionary jurisdiction, to act as a Standing Committee, upon all questions pertaining to the interests thereof; and, in case of the absence of the Bishop from his jurisdiction, or of a vacancy in the Episcopate, said Standing Committee shall be the Ecclesiastical Authority of such missionary jurisdiction.

[7.] Every Bishop elected and consecrated under this Section, or Foreign Missionary Bishop heretofore consecrated, shall report to each General Council his official acts, and the state of the Mission under his supervision.

§ 11. [1.] A Diocese without a Bishop, or of which the Bishop is for the time under a disability by reason of a judicial sentence, may, by its Council, be placed under the full Episcopal charge and authority of the Bishop of another Diocese, or of a Missionary Bishop, who shall by that act be authorized to perform all the duties and offices of the Bishop of the Diocese so vacant or having the Bishop disabled; until, in the case of a vacant Diocese, a Bishop be duly elected and consecrated for the same; and, in the case of a Diocese whose Bishop is disqualified as aforesaid, until the disqualification be removed; or until, in either case, the said act of the Council be revoked. *Canon III. Diocese without a Bishop placed under charge of another Bishop.*

[2.] No Diocese thus placed under the full charge and authority of the Bishop of another Diocese, or a Missionary Bishop, shall invite a second Bishop to perform any Episcopal duty, or exercise authority, till its connection with the first Bishop has expired or is revoked. *No other Bishop to officiate there during such charge.*

§ 12. [1.] If, during the session of the General Council, or within six calendar months before the meeting of any such Council, a Bishop shall desire to resign his jurisdiction, he shall make known in writing to the House of Bishops such his desire, together with the reasons moving him thereto; whereupon the House of Bishops may investigate the whole case of the proposed resignation, including not only the facts and reasons that may be set forth in the application for the proposed resignation, but any other facts and circumstances bearing upon it, so that the whole subject of the propriety or necessity of such resignation may be placed fully before the House of Bishops. *Episcopal resignations. Investigation*

[2.] An investigation having thus been made, the House of Bishops may decide on the application; and, by the vote of a majority of those present, accept or refuse to accept such resignation; and, in all cases of a proposed resignation, the Bishops shall cause their proceedings to be recorded on their journal; and, in case of acceptance, the resignation shall be complete when thus recorded; and notice thereof shall be given to the House of Deputies. *House of Bishops to accept or refuse.*

[3.] In case a Bishop should desire to resign at any period not within six calendar months before the meeting of a General Council, he shall make known to the senior Bishop such his desire, with the reasons moving him thereunto; whereupon the senior Bishop shall communicate, without delay, a copy of the same to every Bishop of this Church having Ecclesiastical jurisdiction within the Confederate States; and also to the Standing Committee of the Diocese *Resignation during recess of General Council.*

to which the Bishop desiring to resign may belong; and, at the same time, summon said Bishops to meet him in person, at a place to be by him designated, and at a time not less than three calendar months from the date of his summons; and, should a number not less than a majority of all the said Bishops meet at the time and place designated, they shall then have all the powers given by the previous clauses of this Section to the House of Bishops; and, should a number less than a majority assemble, they shall have power to adjourn from time to time, until they can secure the attendance of a majority of all the said Bishops. Should

a proposed resignation of a Bishop be accepted at any meeting of the Bishops for that purpose held during a recess, then the senior Bishop present shall pronounce such resignation complete, and communicate the same to the Ecclesiastical Authority of each Diocese, who shall cause the same to be communicated to the several Clergymen in charge of Congregations therein. And it shall be the further duty of the senior Bishop to cause such resignation to be for-

mally recorded on the journal of the House of Bishops that may meet in General Council next thereafter. If the Bishop

desirous of resigning should be the senior Bishop, then all the duties directed in this Section to be performed by the senior Bishop shall devolve upon the Bishop next in seniority.

[4.] No Bishop whose resignation of the Episcopal jurisdiction of a Diocese has been consummated pursuant to this Section, shall be eligible to any Diocese now in union, or which may hereafter be admitted into union, with this Church; but he may perform Episcopal acts at the request of any Bishop of this Church within the limits of his Diocese.

[5.] A Bishop, who ceases to have charge of a Diocese, shall still be subject in all matters to the Canons and authority of the General Council.

[6.] In case a suspended Bishop of this Church should desire to resign at any period not within six calendar months before the meeting of a General Council, he shall make known by letter to the senior Bishop such desire; whereupon the senior Bishop shall communicate a copy of the same to each Bishop of this Church having jurisdiction within the Confederate States; and, in case a majority of such Bishops shall return to the senior Bishop their written assent to such resignation, the same shall be deemed valid

and final; and written information of the said resignation shall at once be communicated by the senior Bishop to the

Bishop and Diocese concerned, and to each Bishop of this
Church. And it shall be the further duty of the senior
Bishop to cause such resignation to be formally recorded
on the journal of the House of Bishops that may meet in
General Council next thereafter.

CANON IV.

OF A LIST OF THE MINISTERS OF THIS CHURCH.

§ 1. The Secretary of the House of Deputies shall keep
a register of all the Clergy of this Church, whose names
shall be delivered to him in the following manner, that is
to say : The Ecclesiastical Authority of this Church, in each
Diocese, shall, at the time of each General Council, deliver
to the said Secretary a list of the names of all the Ministers of this Church in their proper Dioceses, annexing the
names of their respective cures, or of their stations in any
Colleges or other Seminaries of Learning ; or, in regard to
those who have not any cures or other stations, their places
of residence only ; and the said list shall, from time to
time, be published in the journals of the General Council.

Secretary of House of Deputies to keep a Register.

§ 2. The Ecclesiastical Authority of each Diocese shall,
during the intervals between the meetings of the General
Council, take such means of making known the admission
of Ministers among them, as shall tend to prevent ignorant
and unwary people from being imposed on by persons pre-
tending to be authorized Ministers of this Church.

Admission of Ministers to be notified.

CANON V.

OF THE MODE OF SECURING AN ACCURATE VIEW OF THE STATE OF THE CHURCH.

§ 1. As a full and accurate view of the state of the
Church, from time to time, is highly useful and necessary,
it is hereby ordered that every Minister of this Church, or
if the Parish be vacant, the Wardens or Vestry, shall de-

Statement in Parochial Reports.

4

Canon V.

liver, on or before the first day of every Diocesan Council, to the Bishop of the Diocese, or where there is no Bishop, to the President of the Council, a statement of the number of baptisms, confirmations, marriages and funerals, and of the number of communicants in his Parish or Church, also the state and condition of the Sunday Schools in his Parish, also of the amount of the Communion alms, the contributions for Missions, Diocesan, Domestic and Foreign, for Parochial schools, for Church purposes in general, and of all other matters that may throw light on the state of the

Clergymen not settled to report services.

same. And every Clergyman, not regularly settled in any Parish or Church, shall also report the occasional services he may have performed; and, if he have performed no such services, the causes or reasons which have prevented the same. And these reports, or such parts of them as the Bishop shall think fit, may be read in Council, and shall be entered on the journals thereof.

Bishop's Address.

§ 2. At every annual Diocesan Council, the Bishop shall deliver an address, stating the affairs of the Diocese since the last meeting of the Council; the names of the Churches which he has visited; the number of persons confirmed; the names of those who have been received as candidates for Orders, and of those who have been ordained, suspended, or degraded; the changes by death, removal, or otherwise, which have taken place among the Clergy; and, in general, all matters tending to throw light on the affairs of the Diocese; which address shall be inserted on the journals.

Duty of Diocesan Secretaries.

§ 3. The Secretaries of the several Diocesan Councils shall forward to the House of Deputies, at every General Council, the journals of the different Diocesan Councils, Episcopal Charges, Addresses and Pastoral Letters since the last General Council, together with such other papers as may tend to throw light on the state of the Church in

Committee on the state of the Church.

in each Diocese. A Committee shall then be appointed to draw up a view of the state of the Church, and to make report to the House of Deputies; which report, when agreed to by the said House, shall be sent to the House of Bishops, with a request that they will prepare and publish a Pastoral

Pastoral Letter.

Letter to the members of the Church. When any such letter is published, every Clergyman having a Pastoral charge shall read it to his Congregation on some occasion of public worship.

Condensed Report from each Diocese.

§ 4. The Bishop and Standing Committee of the Church in every Diocese, or, if there be no Bishop, the Standing Committee only, shall prepare, previously to the meeting of every General Council, a condensed report, and a tabular view of the state of the Church in their Diocese, comprising therein a summary of the statistics from the parochial reports, and from the Bishop's addresses, specifying the capital and proceeds of the Episcopal fund, and of all benevolent and missionary associations of Churchmen within the Diocese, for the purpose of aiding the Committee on the state of the Church, appointed by the House of Deputies, in drafting their reports.

Canon V.

. . .

CANON VI.

OF THE MODE OF PUBLISHING AUTHORIZED EDITIONS OF THE STANDARD BIBLE OF THIS CHURCH.

The Ecclesiastical Authority in each Diocese of this Church shall appoint, from time to time, some suitable person or persons, to compare and correct all new editions of the Bible by the standard edition agreed upon by the General Council, and a certificate of their having been so compared and corrected shall be published with said book.

Editions of the Bible to be corrected by the Standard.

. . .

CANON VII.

OF PUBLISHING EDITIONS OF THE BOOK OF COMMON PRAYER.

The Ecclesiastical Authority of this Church, in each Diocese, shall appoint one or more Presbyters of the Diocese, who shall compare and correct every new edition of the Book of Common Prayer, the Articles, Offices, Metre Psalms and Hymns, by a copy of the standard edition; and a certificate, specifying the name of the Publishing House and the date of said edition, and that it has been so compared and corrected, shall be published with the same. And in case any edition shall be published without such correction, it shall be the duty of the said Ecclesiastical Authority to give public notice that such edition is not authorized by the Church.

Correct Editions of the Prayer-Book.

Canon VIII.

CANON VIII.

OF PAROCHIAL INSTRUCTION.

Parochial instruc-
tion.

The Ministers of this Church who have charge of parishes or cures, shall not only be diligent in instructing the children in the Catechism, but shall, also, by stated catechetical lectures and instruction, be diligent in informing the youth and others in the Doctrine, Constitution and Liturgy of the Church.

TITLE III.

OF DISCIPLINE.

—··· —

CANON I.

OF AMENABILITY AND OFFENCES FOR WHICH A MINISTER MAY BE TRIED AND PUNISHED.

§ 1. Every Minister shall be amenable for offences committed by him to the Ecclesiastical Authority of the Diocese in which he is canonically resident at the time of the charge. *To whom Ministers amenable.*

§ 2. Every Minister shall be liable to presentment and trial, for any crime or immorality, for disorderly conduct, for drunkenness, for profane swearing, for frequenting places liable to be abused to licentiousnesness, and for violation of the Constitution or Canons of this Church, or of the Diocese to which he belongs ; and, on being found guilty, he shall be admonished, suspended, or degraded, according to the Canons of the Diocese in which the trial takes place. *Punishable offences.*

§ 3. A Clergyman who presents a person to the Bishop for Holy Orders, as specified in the office for Ordination, without having good grounds to believe that the requisitions of the Canons have been complied with, shall be liable to Ecclesiastical censure. *Liability of Clergymen presenting.*

§ 4. If a Minister of this Church shall be accused, by public rumour, of discontinuing all exercise of the ministerial office without lawful cause, or of living in the habitual disuse of public worship or of the Holy Eucharist, according to the offices of this Church, or of being guilty of scandalous, immoral or disorderly conduct, or of violating the Canons, or preaching or inculcating heretical doctrine, it shall be the duty of the Bishop, or, if there be no Bishop, of the Clerical members of the Standing Committee, to see that an inquiry be instituted as to the truth of such public *Proceedings on public rumour.*

Canon I.   rumour. And in case of the individual being proceeded against and convicted according to such rules or process as may be provided by the Councils of the respective Dioceses, he shall be admonished, suspended or degraded, as the nature of the case may require, in conformity with their respective Constitutions and Canons.

CANON II.

TRIAL OF PRESBYTERS AND DEACONS UNDER MISSIONARY JURISDICTION.

Presentment.   § 1. The jurisdiction of this Church extending in right, though not always in form, to all persons belonging to it within the Confederate States and Territories, it is hereby enacted, that each Missionary Bishop shall have jurisdiction over the clergy in the district assigned him, and may, in case a presentment and trial of a clergyman become proper, request the action of any Presbyters and Standing Committee, in any Diocese sufficiently near, and the presentment and trial shall be according to the Constitution and Canons of said Diocese. Or, if there be a Standing Committee appointed by the Missionary Bishop, the clerical members thereof may make presentment, and the trial shall take place according to the Constitution and Canons of any Diocese of this Church which may have been selected at the time of the appointment of such Standing Committee: *Provided,* That the Court shall be composed of at least three Presbyters, excluding the members of the Standing Committee and the accused.

Trials.   § 2. If any Minister of this Church, acting under a Foreign Missionary appointment, and within the jurisdiction of a Foreign Missionary Bishop of this Church, shall commit any offence for which Ministers may be tried and punished, or shall refuse obedience to the lawful authority of the Missionary Bishop, such Clergyman shall be proceeded against according to the Constitution and Canons of any Diocese in this Church, which may have been selected at the time of the appointment of the Standing Committee of such missionary jurisdiction: *Provided,* That a presentment shall first be made by the members of said Standing

Committee, or, if the accused party be a member of the Standing Committee, by the other member or members thereof.

§ 3. The Court for the trial of such Minister shall consist of five Presbyters, excluding the members of the Standing Committee; or, if there be not five, then of all the members of such missionary jurisdiction. If there be more than five, then shall the Standing Committee select, by lot, the five who shall compose the Court, which Court shall proceed in the trial, according to the Canons of the General Council of this Chhurch, so far as the same may be applicable to such a case; and where no provision is made adequate to the exigency, the Court shall consider and adjudge the case according to the principles of law and equity.

§ 4. The sentence of the Court shall be rendered to the Bishop of such missionary jurisdiction, who shall have power to revise and modify the same, and the decision of the Bishop shall be final and conclusive.

Canon II.

The Court.

Sentence.

...

CANON III.

OF A CLERGYMAN IN ONE DIOCESE OR MISSIONARY DISTRICT CHAGEABLE WITH MISDEMEANOR IN ANOTHER.

§ 1. If a Clergyman of this Church, belonging to any Diocese or Missionary District, shall, in any other Diocese or Missionary District, conduct himself in such a way as to be chargeable with misdemeanor, the Ecclesiastical Authority thereof shall give notice of the same to the Ecclesiastical Authority where he is canonically resident, exhibiting, with the information given, reasonable ground for presuming its correctness: If the Ecclesiastical Authority, when thus informed, shall omit, for the space of three months, to proceed against the offending Clergyman, the Ecclesiastical Authority of the Diocese or Missionary District, within which the alleged offence was committed, may institute proceedings, and the decision given shall be conclusive.

Offence committed in a different Diocese.

§ 2. If a Clergyman shall come temporarily into any Diocese, under the imputation of having elsewhere been guilty of any crime or misdemeanor, or if any Clergyman, while sojourning in any Diocese, shall misbehave, the

Bishop may admonish, &c.

Canon III.

Bishop, upon probable cause, may admonish such Clergyman, and ⁘forbid him to officiate in said Diocese. And if, after such prohibition, the said Clergyman so officiate, the Ecclesiastical Authority shall give notice to all the Clergy and Congregations in said Diocese, that the officiating of the said Clergyman is prohibited; and like notice shall be given to the Ecclesiastical Authority of the Diocese to which the said Clergyman belongs. And such prohibition shall continue in force, until the Ecclesiastical Authority of the first named Diocese be satisfied of the innocence of the said Clergyman, or until he be acquitted on trial.

Case of Clergymen ordained in foreign countries.

§ 3. The provisions of the last Section shall apply to Clergymen ordained in foreign countries by Bishops in communion with this Church: *Provided*, That in such case notice of the prohibition shall be given to the Ecclesiastical Authority under whose jurisdiction the Clergyman shall appear to have last been, and also to all the Bishops exercising jurisdiction in this Church.

CANON IV.

OF RENUNCIATION OF THE MINISTRY.

Where no proceeding is pending.

§ 1. If any Minister of this Church, against whom there is no Ecclesiastical proceeding instituted, shall declare, in writing, to the Ecclesiastical Authority to which he belongs, his renunciation of the Ministry, and his design not to officiate in future in any of the offices thereof, said Ecclesiastical Authority shall record the declaration so made. The Bishop shall then depose him from the Ministry, and pronounce and record in the presence of two or more Clergymen, that the person so declaring has been deposed from the Ministry of this Church; and if there be no Bishop in such Diocese, the same sentence may be pronounced by the Bishop of any other Diocese invited by the Standing Committee to attend for that purpose.

Suspension of action.

§ 2. If the Ecclesiastical Authority, to whom such declaration renouncing the Ministry is made, shall have reason to believe that the person has acted unadvisedly and hastily, all action thereupon may be forborne for the space of not more than six months, during which time the person may withdraw his application.

§ 3. If the Bishop shall have ground to suppose the person to be liable to presentment for any canonical offence, he may, in his discretion, and with the consent of the Standing Committee, proceed to have the applicant put upon his trial, notwithstanding his having made the aforesaid declaration; and the same discretion is allowed to the Standing Committee, in case the Diocese should be without a Bishop. Canon IV.

Where liabil'y to presentment.

§ 4. In the case of deposition from the Ministry, as above provided for, the Bishop shall give notice thereof to the Ecclesiastical Authority of every Diocese of this Church; and if the clergyman be deposed for anything involving moral degradation, such notice shall be read before every congregation of the Diocese to which he belongs, on the occasion of public worship next after the reception of such notice. Notice of deposition.

CANON V.

OF THE ABANDONMENT OF THE COMMUNION OF THIS CHURCH BY A PRESBYTER OR DEACON.

§ 1. If any Presbyter or Deacon shall, without availing himself of the provisions of Canon IV. of this Title, abandon the Communion of this Church, either by an open renunciation of the doctrine, discipline, and worship of this Church, or by a formal admission into any religious body not in communion with the same, it shall be the duty of the Standing Committee of the Diocese to make certificate of the fact to the Bishop of the Diocese, or, if there be no Bishop, to the Bishop of an adjacent Diocese; which certificate shall be recorded, and shall be taken and deemed by the Bishop as equivalent to a renunciation of the Ministry by the Minister himself. Notice shall then be given to the said Minister, by the said Bishop receiving the certificate, that unless he shall, within six months after being notified, make declaration that the facts alleged in said certificate are false, he will be deposed from the Ministry of this Church. Abandonment without renunciation.

Certificate.

Notice.

§ 2. And if such declaration be not made within six months as aforesaid, the Bishop shall depose said Minister from the Ministry, and pronounce and record, in the presence of two or more Presbyters, that he has been so deposed. Deposition.

4*

Provided, nevertheless, That if the Minister so renouncing shall transmit to the Bishop receiving the certificate, a retraction of the acts or declarations constituting his offence, the Bishop may, at his discretion, abstain from any further proceedings.

CANON VI.

OF A CLERGYMAN ABSENTING HIMSELF FROM HIS DIOCESE.

When a Clergyman has been absent from the Diocese to which he belongs, during two years, without reasons satisfactory to the Bishop thereof, he shall be required by the Bishop to declare the cause or causes thereof in writing; and if he refuse to give his reasons, or if they be deemed insufficient by the Bishop, the Bishop, after due notification of such insufficiency, may, with the advice and consent of the Clerical Members of the Standing Committee, suspend him from the Ministry; which suspension shall continue until he shall give, in writing, sufficient reasons for his absence, or until he shall renew his residence in his Diocese, or until he shall renounce the Ministry according to Canon IV. of this Title. In the case of such suspension as the above provided for, the Bishop shall give notice thereof to the Ecclesiastical Authority of every Diocese of this Church.

CANON VII.

OF THE ABANDONMENT OF THE COMMUNION OF THE CHURCH BY A BISHOP.

If any Bishop abandon the Communion of this Church, either by openly renouncing its doctrine, discipline and worship, or by formally uniting himself with any religious body not in communion with the same, the Standing Committee of the Diocese shall make certificate of the fact to the Senior Bishop, which certificate shall be recorded, and shall be taken and deemed as equivalent to a renunciation of the Ministry by the Bishop himself.

Notice shall then be given to said Bishop by the Senior Bishop receiving the certificate, that unless he shall, within six months after being notified, make declaration that the facts alleged in said certificate are false, he will be deposed from the Ministry of this Church.

And if such declaration be not made within six months as aforesaid, the Senior Bishop, with the consent of the majority of the Bishops entitled to seats in the House of Bishops, shall depose from the Ministry the Bishop so certified as abandoning, and shall pronounce and record, in the presence of two or more Bishops, that he has been so deposed.

margin notes: Canon VII. Notice to be given. Deposition.

- - • • • -

CANON VIII.

OF THE TRIAL OF A BISHOP.

§ 1. Any Bishop of this Church may be presented for trial on charges for the following offences, viz : (1.) Crime or immorality. (2.) Holding and teaching publicly, or privately and advisedly, any doctrine contrary to that held by the Protestant Episcopal Church in the Confederate States. (3.) Violation of the Constitution or Canons of the General Council. (4.) Violation of the Constitution or Canons of the Diocese to which he belongs. (5.) Any act which involves a breach of his Ordination or Consecration vows.

margin note: Offences for which may be tried.

§ 2. [1.] The proceedings shall commence by charges in writing ; and, except when the charge is holding and teaching doctrine contrary to that held by this Church, shall be signed by either

Five male Communicants of this Church, in good standing, belonging to the Diocese of the accused, of whom two at least must be Presbyters ; or,

By seven male Communicants of this Church, in good standing, of whom two at least shall be Presbyters, and three of which seven shall belong to the Diocese of the accused.

margin note: Charges in writing.

[2.] Whenever a Bishop of this Church shall have reason to believe that there are in circulation rumours, reports, or charges affecting his moral or religious character, he may, if he please, acting in conformity with the written advice and consent of any two of his brother Bishops whom he may select, demand of the Presiding Bishop of the House of Bishops, or if he be the Bishop affected by such rumours,

margin note: Action on rumours.

Canon VIII. or if he be related to him within the degrees hereinafter mentioned, then to the Bishop next in seniority not so related, to convene a Board of Inquiry in the mode hereinafter set forth, to investigate such rumours, reports, and charges, and to proceed, in all respects, according to the provisions of this Canon, as if charges had been formally made in either of the two modes first mentioned in this section.

Lay Advocate. [3.] Whenever charges are formally made in either of the modes first above mentioned, the accusers may, if they choose, select a Lay Communicant of this Church, of the profession of the law, to act as their adviser, advocate and agent, in preparing the accusation, proofs, etc., until such time as a Board of Inquiry is convened in such manner as is hereinafter provided for; or they may prepare such Charges to be certified. charges themselves, without regard to any particular form; and, in either case, the grounds of accusation must be set forth with reasonable certainty of time, place and circumstance.

To whom delivered. § 3. The charges, having been prepared in either of the modes first above mentioned, shall then be delivered to the Presiding Bishop of this Church, if he be not the accused, nor related to the accused in any degree mentioned hereinafter in this Canon; in either of which cases, the charges shall be delivered to the next Bishop in seniority not so related.

Board of Inquiry. § 4. A Board for making a preliminary inquiry into charges thus preferred, shall be constituted as follows, whenever such Board shall be necessary, viz:

How constituted. [1.] The Presiding Bishop, or senior Bishop, as the case may be, to whom such charges are delivered, shall take the list of Deputies to the last General Council that was held before such charges were presented, and from that list shall choose by lot two Presbyters and two Laymen from the deputation of the Diocese of the accused, and two Presbyters and two Laymen from each of the respective deputations of the three Dioceses adjoining that of the accused; and if there be not three adjoining, of the three nearest thereto; and if more than three Dioceses adjoin that of the accused, those three that have the largest number of canonically-resident Presbyters in them shall be accounted adjoining, for the purposes of this Canon; and the sixteen individuals thus selected by lot shall constitute the Board of Inquiry, a majority of whom shall form a quorum for doing business.

[2.] The Presiding Bishop, or next in seniority as the case may be, immediately after thus selecting by lot the Board of Inquiry, shall give notice thereof to each member of said Board, and direct him to attend at a time and place designated by him, and organize the Board; and it shall be the duty of each member so to attend. The place must be within the Diocese of the accused. The Presiding Bishop shall, at the same time, send a copy of the charges to the senior Presbyter of those thus selected by lot from the four Dioceses.

[3.] On assembling, the Board shall organize by choosing from among themselves a President and Secretary, and shall also appoint a Church Advocate, who must be a Lay Communicant of this Church, and of the profession of the law, and who thenceforward shall, in all stages of the proceedings, if a trial be ordered, represent the Church, and be the party on the one hand, while the accused is the party on the other. The sittings of the Board shall be private; the Church Advocate shall not attend as prosecuting counsel, but shall be at all times at hand and in readiness to give his advice in all questions submitted to him by the Board.

[4.] In conducting the investigation, the Board shall hear the accusations and such proof as the accusers may produce, and shall determine whether, upon matters of law and of fact, as presented to them, there is sufficient ground to put the accused Bishop upon his trial; and in such investigation, as well as in all cases of trial by an Ecclesiastical Court now authorized, or hereafter to be authorized, by the Constitution or Canons of the General Council, the laws of the State in which such investigation or trial is had, so far as they relate to the law of evidence, shall be adopted and taken as the rules by which the said Board or Court shall be governed. If a majority of the Board present on such investigation shall be of opinion that there are sufficient grounds to put the accused Bishop upon his trial, they shall direct the Church Advocate to prepare a presentment, to be signed by such of the Board as agree thereto; and to that end, shall place in his hands all the charges, together with the testimony that has been laid before the Board.

[5.] The Board shall then direct the Church Advocate to transmit to the Bishop from whom they received the charges, the presentment thus signed; and shall cause him also, without delay, to send to the accused Bishop a copy of the same, certified by the Church Advocate to be correct.

Canon VIII.

Notice to Members.

Place of meeting.

Copy of charges.

Organization of Board.

Sittings private.

Duty of the Board.

Law of evidence.

Presentment.

To whom to be sent.

[6.] If a majority of the Board present shall be of opinion that there is not sufficient ground to put the accused Bishop upon his trial, in such case, the charges, together with a *Refusal to present.* certificate of the President of the Board of its refusal to make a presentment, shall be sent to the Secretary of the House of Bishops, to be deposited among the archives of that House. *Bar to future presentment.* And no proceedings shall thereafter be had by *Exception.* way of presentment on such charges, except upon the affidavit of a respectable Communicant of the Church, of the discovery of new testimony as to the facts charged, and setting forth what such testimony is.

Limitation of time. [7.] No presentment shall be found in any case, unless the alleged offence shall have been committed within five years next before the day on which the charges were delivered to the Presiding or senior Bishop. But if the accused *Conviction in a State Court.* shall have been convicted of the alleged offence in a State court, notwithstanding five years may have elapsed since its commission, a presentment may be founded on charges delivered to the Presiding or senior Bishop at any time within one year after such conviction.

Notice to accused on presentment. §5. [1.] When a presentment has been made by the Board of Inquiry, or a majority thereof, to the Bishop from whom they received the charges, it shall be the duty of such Bishop forthwith to give to the accused written notice to attend, at some place not more than one hundred miles from the place of residence of the accused Bishop, and at some time not less than twenty days after the time of serving such notice, either personally, or by some agent authorized by him in writing to act for him in the premises, for the purpose of selecting the Bishops who shall form the Court for the *And to Church Advocate.* trial of the said accused Bishop upon the said presentment. He shall also give notice to the Church Advocate of the time and place appointed for such selection.

Formation of Court. [2.] At the time and place appointed in the notices, the Bishop who has given the notices shall attend; and, in the presence of the accused Bishop, or of his agent authorized as aforesaid, and also in the presence of the Church Advocate, or of such person or persons as may attend in his behalf, or, if no person shall attend on behalf of one or both, of two Presbyters named by himself, the said Bishop shall cause to be placed in a vessel the names of all the Bishops of this Church entitled to seats in the House of Bishops, then being within the territory of the Confederate States, except the accused and those Bishops who may be related to him either by consanguinity or affinity, in the

direct ascending or descending line, or as brother, uncle, or
nephew. He shall then cause seven of the said names to
be drawn. The names so drawn shall be entered upon a
list as they are drawn, and the accused or his agent may
strike off the list one name, and the said Church Advocate
or his agent another name, and so as to reduce the number
to five. If it shall happen that either party shall neglect or
refuse to strike, then the Bishop who has given the notices
shall reduce the number to five, by striking off so many of
the last drawn names as will reduce the list to that number.
The five Bishops whose names remain, or a majority of
them, when assembled, shall constitute the Court for the
trial of the accused upon the presentment.

[3.] The Court having been thus constituted, the Bishop
to whom the presentment was made shall immediately communicate to each Bishop who has thus been by lot designated as one of the triers, the fact that he is a member of the
Court. He shall appoint a time and place for the assembling of the Court. The time shall not be less than two
nor more than six calendar months from the day on which
the notice should arrive at the most distant Diocese, in the
ordinary course of the public mail. The place shall be
within the Diocese or Missionary field of the accused Bishop,
unless where the same may be of such difficult access, in
the judgment of the Presiding or senior Bishop, that reasonable convenience may require the appointment of another
location. And the said senior Bishop shall cause the Church
Advocate to send certified copies of the said presentment
to all the Bishops who constitute the Court.

[4.] The Bishop to whom the presentment has been made
shall also immediately communicate to the accused the
names of the members of the Court, and inform him of the
time and place appointed for its meeting, and summon him
then and there to appear and answer. He or any other
Bishop of this Church having charge of a Diocese, shall
have power, until the Court assembles, upon the application
of either the Church Advocate or the accused, to issue a
summons for witnesses.

§ 6. The Bishops who constitute the Court, or a majority
of them, having assembled according to the notice given
them, which notice it is hereby made their duty to obey,
shall proceed as follows, viz:

[1.] They shall elect a President out of their own number, and appoint a Presbyter of the Church as Clerk, and if
necessary, another Presbyter as Assistant Clerk; and when

Canon VIII.

Reading of presentment.

thus organized, the President shall direct the Clerk to call the names of the Church Advocate and the accused; and if both appear, he shall then cause the Clerk to read the presentment which was delivered to the Presiding or senior Bishop, whose duty it is hereby made to deliver the same to the Court upon its organization.

Call to plead.

[2.] The accused shall then be called upon by the Court to say whether he is guilty or not guilty of the offence or offences charged against him, and his plea shall be duly recorded; and on his neglect or refusal to plead, the plea of not guilty shall be entered for him, and the trial shall

Provisos.

proceed: *Provided,* That, for sufficient cause, the Court may adjourn from time to time; and *Provided, also,* That the accused shall, at all times during the trial, have liberty to be present, and in due time and order produce his testimony, and to make his defence.

Non-appearance.

[3.] If the accused neglect or refuse to appear in person, according to the notice served on him as aforesaid, except for some reasonable cause to be allowed by the Court, they

Contumacy.

shall proceed to pronounce him in contumacy, and notify him that sentence of suspension or degradation will be pronounced against him by the Court at the expiration of

Three months' grace.

three months, unless within that time he tender himself ready, and accordingly appear to take his trial on the presentment. But if the accused shall not tender himself before the expiration of the said three months, sentence of suspension or degradation from the Ministry may be pronounced against him by the Court.

Common Law the rule of proceeding.

[4.] The accused being present, and the trial proceeding, it shall be conducted according to the principles of the Common Law, as the same are generally administered in the Confederate States; nor shall any testimony be received at the trial, except from witnesses who have signed a declaration in the following words, to be read aloud before the witness testifies, and to be filed with the records of the Court:

Declaration of witness.

" I, A. B., a witness summoned to testify on the trial of a presentment against the Right Rev. ———, a Bishop of the Protestant Episcopal Church in the Confederate States, now pending, do most solemnly call God to witness that the evidence I am about to give shall be the truth, the whole truth, and nothing but the truth; so help me God!"

Deposition.

And if it be necessary to take the testimony of an absent witness on a commission, such testimony shall be preceded by a similar written declaration of the witness, which shall be filed and transmitted with his or her deposition to the

Court. The testimony of each witness shall be reduced to Canon VIII.
writing. And in case there is ground to suppose that the
attendance of any witness on the trial cannot be obtained,
it shall be lawful for either party to apply to the Court if in
session, or if not, to any member thereof, who shall thereupon appoint a commissary to take the deposition of such Commissary.
witness; and such party so desiring to take the deposition,
shall give to the other party reasonable notice of the time
and place of taking such deposition, accompanying such
notice with the interrogatories to be propounded to the
witness; whereupon it shall be lawful for the other party,
within six days after such notice, to propound cross-inter- Cross-Examina-
tion.
rogatories; and such interrogatories and cross-interrogato-
ries, if any be propounded, shall be sent to the commissary,
who shall thereupon proceed to take the testimony of such
witness, upon oath or affirmation, and transmit it under
seal to the Court. But no deposition shall be read at the On what condition depositions to
be read.
trial, unless the Court have reasonable assurance that the
attendance of the witness cannot be procured, or unless
both parties shall consent that it may be read. *Provided,* Proviso.
That in any Diocese in which the civil government has
authorized the Ecclesiastical Courts therein to issue summons for witnesses, or to administer an oath, the Court
shall act in conformity to such laws.

[5.] All notices and papers may be served by a summoner Service of notices
and papers.
or summoners, to be appointed by the Court when the same
is in session, or by a member thereof; and the certificate of
any such summoner shall be evidence of the due service of
a notice or paper. In case of service by any other person,
the fact may be proved by the affidavit of such person.
The delivery of a written notice or paper to the accused Certificate of
service.
party, or to the Church Advocate, or leaving it, or a copy
thereof, at the residence, or last known residence, of either,
shall be deemed sufficient service of such notice or paper,
on the Church Advocate and accused respectively. If the
person to be served with any notice or paper shall have left
the Confederate States, it shall be a sufficient service thereof
to leave a copy of such notice or paper at his last place of
abode within the Confederate States, sixty days before the
day on which the appearance, or other act required by the
said notice or paper, is to be performed.

[6.] The accused party may, if he think proper, have the Accused may
have counsel.
aid of counsel; and if he should choose to have more than
one counsel, the Church Advocate may have assistant

5

Canon VIII.
advocates, to be named by the accusers; but in every case
the Court may regulate the number of counsel who shall
address the Court or examine witnesses. The Church

Counsel to be Communicants.
Advocate shall be considered the party on one side, and the
accused on the other. All counsel must be Communicants
of the Church.

Opinion of Court.
[7.] The Court, having fully heard the allegations and
proofs of the parties, and deliberately considered the same,
after the parties have withdrawn, shall declare respectively,
whether, in their opinion, the accused is guilty or not
guilty of each particular charge and specifications contained in the presentment, in the order in which they are
set forth; and the accused shall be considered as not guilty
of every charge and specification of which he shall not be
pronounced guilty by a majority of the members of the
Court.

Decision.
[8.] The decision of the Court as to all the charges and
specifications of which a majority of the members of the
Court have found him guilty, shall be reduced to writing,
and signed by those who assent to it; and a decision pro-
nouncing him not guilty of all those charges and specifications of which a majority shall not have pronounced him
guilty, shall also be drawn up, and signed by those who
assent to it; and the decision thus signed shall be regarded
as the judgment of the Court, and shall be pronounced in
the presence of the parties, if they shall think proper to
attend.

Accused to be heard.
[9.] If the accused shall be found guilty of any charge
or specification, the Court shall proceed to ask him whether
he has anything to say before the sentence is passed, and
may, in their discretion, give him time to prepare what he
wishes to say, and appoint a time for passing the sentence;
and before passing sentence, the Court may adjourn from
time to time, and give the accused reasonable opportunity
of showing cause to induce a belief that justice has not

New trial.
been done, or that he has discovered new testimony; and
the Court, or a majority of its members, may, according
to a sound discretion, grant him a new trial. Before
passing sentence, the accused shall always have the opportunity of being heard, if he have aught to say in excuse or
palliation.

Sentence.
[10.] The accused having been heard, or not desiring to
be heard, the sentence of the Court shall then be pronounced, and shall be either admonition, suspension as

defined by the existing Canons of this Church, or degra- Canon VIII.
dation, as the offence or offences adjudged to be proved
shall seem to deserve. It shall be the duty of the Court,
whenever sentence has been pronounced, whether it be
upon a trial, or for contumacy, to communicate such sentence to the Ecclesiastical Authority of every Diocese of
this Church; and it shall be the duty of such Authority to Sentence to be communicated.
cause such sentence to be made known to every Clergyman
under his jurisdiction.

[11.] Every Court shall keep a full record of its proceed- Record.
ings, including the whole evidence given before it. Should
any Court refuse to insert in its record a statement of any
testimony which has been received, or of any decision which
the Court has made, or of any fact which has occurred in
Court, or any paper which either party has produced, it
shall be the right of either party to file an exception in Exceptions.
writing, containing a statement of such evidence, decision
or fact, or referring to or describing such paper, which
paper shall also be filed with the exception. All exceptions
and papers so filed shall become parts of the record.

[12.] Such records shall be kept by the Clerk, and in- How kept and attested.
serted in a book, to be attested by the signatures of the
President and Clerk. Every such book, and all papers
connected with any trial, shall be deposited with the Registrar of the General Council. Such books and papers shall
be open to the inspection of every member of this Church.

[13.] Every Court, constituted under the authority of Lay advisers.
this Canon, may be attended by one or more Lay advisers,
who shall be Communicants of this Church, and of the
profession of the law. Such advisers may be present at all
the proceedings of the Court, but they shall have no vote
in any case whatever; it shall be their duty to give in person to the Court an opinion on any question not theological,
upon which the Court, or any member thereof, or either
party, shall desire an opinion. If a dispute shall arise
whether any question be or be not theological, it shall be
decided by the Court by a majority of votes. The Court
may always, by unanimous consent, appoint an adviser
or advisers. If they are not unanimous, each member
of the Court may name a candidate; if not more than
three are named, they all shall be advisers; if more
than three are named, the Court shall reduce them to
three by lot.

§ 7. [1.] Any Bishop of this Church may be presented Presentment for erroneous doctrine.

for holding and teaching doctrine inconsistent with that of this Church, by any Bishop in communion with this Church, and not under suspension or degradation. No Bishop shall be presented in any other mode for this offence; and it shall not be lawful for two or more persons to unite in any such presentment. The Bishop making such presentment shall appoint a Church Advocate.

To whom addressed.

[2.] Every presentment for alleged erroneous doctrine shall be signed by the person making it, and shall be addressed to the Bishops of the Protestant Episcopal Church in the Confederate States, and delivered to the senior Bishop entitled to a seat in the House of Bishops, and not being the accused or the accuser, whose duty it shall

Court.

be to convene a Court for the trial of the accused. The Court shall be composed of all the Bishops entitled to seats in the House of Bishops, except the accuser and the accused. Three-fourths of such Bishops shall constitute a

Quorum,

quorum; but the consent of two-thirds of all the Bishops entitled to seats in the House of Bishops shall be necessary

Number to convict.

to a conviction.

Charges against Missionary Bishop.

§ 8. [1.] If charges be preferred against a Missionary Bishop, who is not a Diocesan, such Missionary Bishop shall be required by the Presiding or senior Bishop to name some one of the three Dioceses nearest to his District or Missionary field; and such selection having been made, the proceedings shall then be precisely such as, under this Canon, they would be were he the Diocesan of the Diocese named by him. Should the Missionary Bishop refuse to name a Diocese, then the Presiding Bishop may name any one of the three above designated, and the effect shall be the same as if the nomination had been made by the accused Missionary Bishop.

Bishop without jurisdiction.

[2.] If charges be preferred against a Bishop having no jurisdiction, he shall be proceeded against precisely as if he were the Diocesan of the Diocese in which he has his civil residence.

Mode of trying.

[3.] Any Foreign Missionary Bishop shall, on presentment by two-thirds of the Missionaries under his charge, for immorality or heresy, or for a violation of the Constitution or Canons of this Church, be tried, and, if found guilty, sentenced, in all particulars as if he were actually resident within the limits of the Confederate States, except that the trial may be within any Diocese in the Confederate States.

CANON IX.

OF SENTENCES.

§ 1. Whenever the penalty of suspension shall be inflicted on a Bishop, Priest or Deacon in this Church, the sentence shall specify on what terms, or at what time, said penalty shall cease.

§ 2. [1.] When any Minister is degraded from the Holy Ministry, he is degraded therefrom entirely, and not from a higher to a lower Order of the same. No degraded or deposed Minister shall be restored to the Ministry.

[2.] Whenever a Clergyman shall be degraded or deposed, the Bishop who pronounces sentence shall, without delay, give notice thereof to the Ecclesiastical Authority of every Diocese, and to each Minister, (or to the Vestry, if there be no Minister,) of the Diocese to which the degraded or deposed Minister belongs, in which notice it shall be stated whether or no the degradation or deposition be for causes affecting his moral character; and each Minister in said Diocese shall give notice thereof to his congregation on the first occasion of public worship next occurring.

------•••------

CANON X.

OF THE REMISSION OR MODIFICATION OF JUDICIAL SENTENCES ON BISHOPS.

The Bishops of this Church, who are entitled to seats in the House of Bishops, may altogether remit and terminate any judicial sentence imposed by Bishops acting collectively as a judicial tribunal; or modify the same so far as to designate a precise period of time, or other specific contingency, on the occurrence of which, such sentence shall utterly cease, and be of no further force or effect: *Provided,* That no such remission or modification shall be made except at a meeting of the House of Bishops, during the session of some General Council, or at a special meeting of the said Bishops, which shall be convened by the Presiding Bishop on the application of any five Bishops; three months' notice in writing, of the time, place and object of the meeting being given to each Bishop, or sent to his usual place of abode:

Canon X.
Majority assenting.

Provided, also, That such remission or modification be assented to by a number of said Bishops not less than a majority of the whole number entitled at the time to seats in the House of Bishops; *and provided,* That nothing herein shall be construed to alter the effect of Canon IX. of this Title.

CANON XI.

REGULATIONS RESPECTING THE LAITY.

Removal of Communicants.

§ 1. A Communicant removing from one Parish to another, shall procure from the Rector of the Parish of his last residence, or, if there be no Rector, from one of the Wardens, a certificate stating that he or she is a Communicant in good standing; and the Rector of the Parish or Congregation to which he or she removes shall not be required to receive him or her as a Communicant until such letter be produced.

Bishop to be informed.

§ 2. As one of the rubrics of this Church requires that every Minister repelling from the Communion shall give an account of the same to the Ordinary, it is hereby provided, that, information of the same being laid before the Ordinary, that is the Bishop, it shall not be his duty to institute an inquiry, unless there be a complaint made to him in writing by the repelled party. But on receiving complaint,

Inquiry on complaint.

the Bishop shall institute an inquiry, as may be directed by the Canons of the Diocese in which the event has taken place; and the notice, given as above by the Minister, shall be a sufficient presentation of the party repelled.

Lay Readers.

§ 3. Persons desiring to act habitually as Lay Readers may do so with the consent of the Ecclesiastical Authority of the Diocese in which they are thus to read.

TITLE IV.

OF THE ORGANIZED BODIES AND OFFICERS OF THE CHURCH.

————•••————

CANON I.

OF THE GENERAL COUNCIL.

§ 1. [1.] The right of calling special meetings of the General Council shall be in the Bishops. This right shall be exercised by the Presiding Bishop, or, in case of his death, by the Bishop who, according to the rules of the House of Bishops, is to preside at the next General Council: *Provided*, That the summons shall be with the consent, or on the requisition of a majority of the Bishops, expressed to him in writing. <small>Special meetings.</small>

[2.] The place of holding any Special Council shall be that selected by the preceding General Council for the meeting of the next General Council, unless circumstances shall render a meeting at such a place unsafe; in which case, the Presiding Bishop may appoint some other place. <small>Place.</small>

[3.] The Deputies elected to the preceding General Council shall be the Deputies at such Special Council, unless in those cases in which other Deputies shall have been chosen in the meantime by any of the Diocesan Councils, and then such other Deputies shall represent in the Special Council the Church of the Diocese in which they have been chosen. <small>Same Deputies.</small>

§ 2. [1.] The journals, files, papers, reports and other documents, which, under Canon V. of Title II., entitled *Of Securing an Accurate View of the State of the Church*, or in any other manner, shall become the property of either House of the General Council of this Church, shall be committed to the keeping of a Presbyter to be elected by the House of Deputies, upon nomination of the House of Bishops, who shall be known as the Registrar of the General Council. <small>Registrar.</small>

[2.] It shall be the duty of the said Registrar to procure all such journals, files, papers, reports and other documents <small>His duties.</small>

now in existence; to arrange, label, file, index and otherwise put in order, and provide for the safe keeping of the same, and all such others as may hereafter come into his possession, in fire-proof box or boxes, in some safe and accessible place of deposit, and to hold the same under such regulations and restrictions as the General Council may from time to time provide.

[3.] It shall be the duty of the said Registrar to procure a proper book of record, and to enter therein a record of the consecrations of all the Bishops of this Church, designating accurately the time and place of the same, with the names of the consecrating Bishops, and of others present and assisting; to have the same authenticated in the fullest manner practicable; and to take care for the similar record and authentication of all future consecrations in this Church.

[4.] The expenses necessary for the purposes contemplated by this section shall be provided for by vote of the General Council, and defrayed by the Treasurer of the same.

§ 3. The Secretary of the House of Deputies, whenever any alteration of the Constitution is proposed, or any other subject submitted to the consideration of the several Diocesan Councils, shall give a particular notice thereof to the Ecclesiastical Authority of this Church in every Diocese.

§ 4. At every triennial meeting of the General Council, a Treasurer shall be chosen by the House of Deputies and confirmed by the House of Bishops, who shall remain in office until the next stated Council, and until a successor be appointed. It shall be his duty to receive and disburse all moneys collected under the authority of the Council, and of which the collection and disbursement shall not otherwise be regulated; and to invest, from time to time, for the benefit of the Council, such surplus funds as he may have on hand. His account shall be rendered triennially to the Council, and shall be examined by a Committee acting under its authority. In case of a vacancy in the office of

Treasurer, it shall be supplied by an appointment to be made by the Ecclesiastical Authority of the Diocese to which he belonged; and the person so appointed shall continue to act until an appointment be made by the Council.

§ 5. In order that the contingent expenses of the General Council may be defrayed, the Several Diocesan Councils shall forward to the Treasurer of the General Council, at or before any meeting thereof, five dollars for each Clergyman within such Diocese.

CANON II.

CANON II.

OF STANDING COMMITTEES.

§ 1. In every Diocese there shall be a Standing Committee, to be appointed by the Council thereof, whose duties, except so far as provided for by the Canons of the General Council, may be prescribed by the Canons of the respective Dioceses. They shall elect from their own body a President and a Secretary. They may meet on their own adjournment from time to time; and the President shall have power to summon special meetings whenever he shall deem it necessary.

§ 2. In every Diocese where there is a Bishop, the Standing Committee shall be a Council of Advice to the Bishop. They shall be summoned on the requisition of the Bishop, whenever he shall wish for their advice. And they may meet of their own accord, and agreeably to their own rules, when they may be disposed to advise the Bishop.

CANON III.

OF CONGREGATIONS AND PARISHES.

No congregation within one Diocese shall unite itself with any other Diocese, and every congregation of this Church shall belong to the Diocese within which their Church building is located.

TITLE V.

MISCELLANEOUS PROVISIONS.

···

CANON I.

OF REPEALED CANONS

Repeal of repealing not re-enact. Whenever there shall be a repealing clause in any Canon, and the said Canon shall be repealed, such repeal shall not be a re-enactment of the Canon or Canons repealed by the said repealing clause.

···

CANON II.

OF THE REPEAL, AMENDMENT AND ENACTMENT OF CANONS.

Form of altering Canons. In all cases of future enactment, the same, if by way of amendment of an existing provision, shall be in the following form: "Canon —— (or Section —— of Canon ——, or Clause —— of Section —— of Canon ——) of Title ——, is hereby amended so as to read as follows:" And if the enactment is of an additional Clause, Section or Canon, it shall be designated as the next Canon, or next Section, or next Clause, of a Canon, or Section, in the order of numbering, of the Title to which the subject properly belongs; and if a Canon or Section or Clause be stricken out, the existing numbering shall be retained, until a new edition of the Canons be directed.

The Committee on Canons of each House of the General Council shall, at the close of each Session, appoint two of their number to certify the changes, if any, made in the Canons, and to report the same, with the proper arrangement thereof, to the Secretary, who shall print the same in the Journal